SCHIRMER'S LIBRARY
OF MUSICAL CLASSICS

Vol. 1057

FRANZ LISZT

Concerto No. 1
In E♭ major
For the Piano

Edited and Revised by

RAFAEL JOSEFFY

Two-Piano Score

G. SCHIRMER, Inc.

DISTRIBUTED BY

HAL•LEONARD®
CORPORATION
7777 W. BLUEMOUND RD. P.O. BOX 13819 MILWAUKEE, WI 53213

Henry Litolff zugeeignet.

Concerto No 1.

Edited and revised by
Rafael Joseffy.

Franz Liszt.

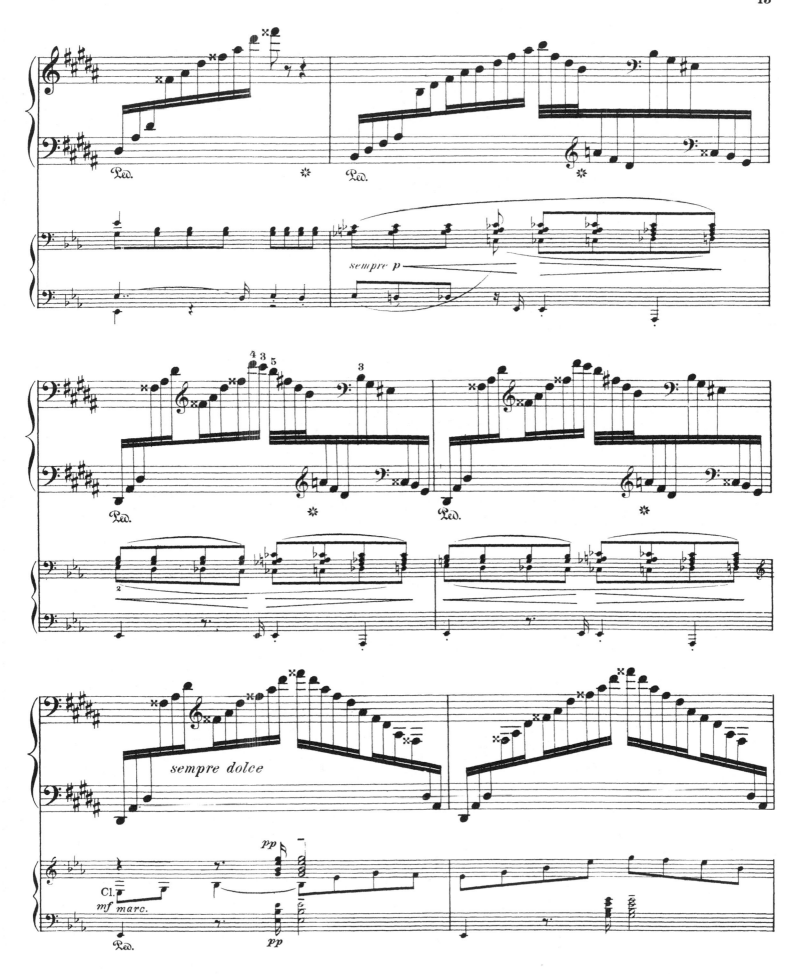

Allegretto vivace.

*) Mark the rhythm of the first motive crisply and sharply.

**) Or, left hand as before.

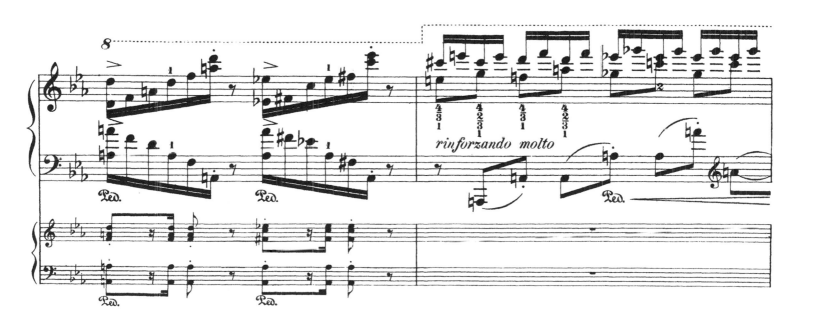

*) or: 𝄢♭ ▬ etc.